ANOINTED
EVEN IN THE GRAVE

The God Who Works Beyond Death

(And it came to pass, as they were burying a man, that, behold, they spied a band of men; and they cast the man into the sepulchre of Elisha: and when the man was let down, and touched the bones of Elisha, he revived, and stood up on his feet. – 2 Kings 13:21 - KJV)

PASTOR DR. CLAUDINE BENJAMIN

For more information or to book an event, contact: inspiredtowinsouls@gmail.com

Published by:

Editor: Cleveland O. McLeish (Author C. Orville McLeish)

ISBN: 978-1-965635-63-6 (paperback)

AUTHOR BIO

Pastor Claudine Benjamin is a prophetic voice and kingdom builder whose ministry carries a deep burden for revival, discipleship, and the great commission. Known for her uncompromising stand on God's Word and her passion to see lives transformed by the power of the Holy Spirit, she ministers with authority, compassion, and a prophetic edge.

Pastor Claudine has been called to equip believers to walk in their God-given identity, to cultivate anointing that lasts, and to pass a spiritual legacy to future generations. Her messages are saturated with scripture, rich in revelation, and designed to awaken a sleeping church to the urgency of the hour.

Through preaching, teaching, writing, and mentoring, she carries a mandate to ignite a fresh hunger for God's presence in every heart she touches. Her greatest desire is to be remembered not for her name, but for the God she served—and for the legacy of lives awakened, empowered, and forever changed by His Spirit.

DEDICATION

I dedicate this work to the One who anointed me, sustained me, and called me to speak His Word with boldness—my Lord and Savior, Jesus Christ. Without His Spirit, there is no oil; without His presence, there is no power; without His grace, there is no hope.

To every believer who has been called to carry the mantle of God's presence—may you live so surrendered that your life will still speak long after you are gone.

And to the next generation, who will rise and run with the fire of God—may you take the oil, guard it, and pour it out without fear.

ACKNOWLEDGMENT

I give all glory and honor to God, who is the Author of this message and the Keeper of my soul. His hand has guided every page, every scripture, and every prophetic thought.

I acknowledge the influence of those spiritual fathers and mothers in the faith who, like Elijah to Elisha, have mentored, corrected, and encouraged me to remain faithful to the call. Your prayers, counsel, and example have shaped me more than you know.

To my family, who have walked beside me with love, patience, and unwavering support—you are part of every assignment God has given me. Your prayers have been the oil that kept the flame burning.

To every pastor, intercessor, evangelist, and believer who refuses to compromise the truth of God's Word—you are living proof that the anointing still flows in our day.

Finally, to the reader—thank you for opening your heart to this message. I pray that as you turn these pages, the Spirit of God will ignite a fresh hunger in you to live and die under His anointing, leaving a legacy that echoes into eternity.

TABLE OF CONTENTS

INTRODUCTION

THE ANOINTING THAT OUTLIVES YOU

Key Scripture

> "And it came to pass, as they were burying a man, that, behold, they spied a band of men; and they cast the man into the sepulchre of Elisha: and when the man was let down, and touched the bones of Elisha, he revived, and stood up on his feet." – 2 Kings 13:21 (KJV)

Some stories in scripture are so startling, so unusual, that they demand we stop and pay attention. The miracle of Elisha's bones is one of those stories. Buried for years, his flesh long gone, Elisha's body was reduced to nothing but dry bones. Yet when a dead man's body touched those bones, life surged through him, and he stood up on his feet.

It's a moment unlike anything else in the Bible—no prayer, no command, no living prophet present—just the lingering residue of God's power on a man who had walked faithfully with Him. It's a reminder that the anointing is not bound by time, circumstance, or even death.

The Grave Cannot Cancel the Anointing

In our natural minds, death marks the end. The body ceases, the voice is silenced, and influence fades. But in the kingdom of God, there is something greater at work. The anointing—God's divine empowerment for His purpose—does not die when the vessel does.

Elisha's bones tell us:

- The anointing is not man-made, so man cannot end it.
- God's power remains effective, even when the vessel is gone.
- Your spiritual influence can outlive your physical presence.

   "For the gifts and calling of God are without repentance." – Romans 11:29 (KJV)

Why This Story Matters Today

We live in a generation obsessed with the temporary—quick results, instant recognition, and self-promotion. Yet the call of God is to build something eternal, something that will still be speaking when our name is forgotten.

This is why the story of Elisha's bones matters now more than ever. It's not about a strange Old Testament miracle—it's about the kind of life you choose to live. Will you live in such a way that your prayers, example, obedience, and faith leave a spiritual deposit for generations to come?

Living for a Legacy, Not Applause

Elisha didn't live for fame—he lived for God. From his first step of obedience, leaving the plow to follow Elijah (**see 1 Kings 19:19–21**), to his last days as a prophet to kings and nations, he was faithful. And that faithfulness left a legacy so saturated with God's presence that even his bones carried power.

Your life is speaking to those around you now. But the greater question is: *Will it still speak when you are gone?*

> **"Blessed are the dead which die in the Lord... that they may rest from their labours; and their works do follow them." – Revelation 14:13 (KJV)**

A Prophetic Call

This book is a prophetic call to:

- Live fully yielded to the Holy Spirit.
- Cultivate an anointing that cannot be buried.
- Pass your faith to the next generation.
- Believe God for resurrection power in hopeless situations.
- Leave behind a legacy that continues to bring glory to God.

Elisha's story challenges us not to waste the anointing on temporary pursuits, but to invest it in things that will outlast us.

What to Expect in These Pages

As you journey through the chapters ahead, you will see:

- How the anointing works, where it comes from, and why it endures.
- Lessons from Elisha's life that can shape your walk with God.
- How to build a spiritual legacy that impacts future generations.
- A prophetic picture of revival in the last days—even in "graveyard" places.

This is more than history—it's an invitation to live in such a way that when your race is over, the anointing on your life will still be producing fruit for the kingdom.

When the dead man touched Elisha's bones, he didn't just come alive—he became a testimony. And so will you, if you choose to live in the fullness of God's calling.

The grave cannot silence the voice of a life lived for God.

The grave cannot cancel the power of the anointing.

And the grave cannot stop the legacy of a surrendered servant.

Live anointed. Die anointed. And let your bones speak.

PART I

THE GOD WHO WORKS BEYOND DEATH

CHAPTER 1

THE GRAVE CANNOT CANCEL THE ANOINTING

Key Scripture

> **"And it came to pass, as they were burying a man, that, behold, they spied a band of men; and they cast the man into the sepulchre of Elisha: and when the man was let down, and touched the bones of Elisha, he revived, and stood up on his feet." – 2 Kings 13:21 (KJV)**

The scene in **2 Kings 13** is both mysterious and awe-inspiring. Elisha, the prophet who had walked in double the anointing of Elijah (**see 2 Kings 2:9–15**), had died and was buried. Years passed. His flesh had long since decayed, and only his bones remained in the tomb. Yet one ordinary day, amid a hurried burial caused by a surprise enemy attack, something extraordinary happened—something that defies human reasoning but aligns perfectly with the nature of God.

The mourners, caught off guard by the approach of a Moabite raiding party, needed to dispose of the body quickly. They threw the corpse into the nearest tomb—the tomb of Elisha. The dead man's body landed on the bones of the prophet, and instantly, life surged back into him. He stood to his feet, alive again.

This miracle declares a profound truth: The anointing of God cannot be confined by the grave. Death may claim the vessel, but it cannot touch the eternal power of the Spirit that once flowed through it. Elisha's bones still carried the residue of God's power, a living testimony to the reality that the anointing is not man-made, not time-bound, and not subject to decay.

The Nature of the Anointing

The anointing is God's empowerment for His purpose. In the Old Testament, the oil poured on kings, priests, and prophets symbolized the Spirit's consecration (**see Exodus 29:7; 1 Samuel 16:13**). But the anointing is more than symbolism—it is the tangible operation of the Holy Spirit working through a human vessel to accomplish God's will.

When God anoints a person, He sets them apart, equips them, and fills them with His divine ability. The source of the anointing is not the human vessel; the vessel simply carries what belongs to God. This is why the grave could not cancel Elisha's anointing—it didn't originate from him; it originated from the Eternal One.

> **"For the gifts and calling of God are without repentance." – Romans 11:29 (KJV)**

The power of God upon Elisha's life was not limited to his earthly years. The grave may end our human activities, but it does not erase the work God has already accomplished through us or the spiritual residue left behind.

Legacy That Lives Beyond You

Elisha's life had been one of obedience, faith, and prophetic authority. He had healed waters (**see 2 Kings 2:19–22**), multiplied oil for a widow (**see 2 Kings 4:1–7**), raised the Shunammite's son from the dead (**see 2 Kings 4:32–37**), fed a multitude (**see 2 Kings 4:42–44**), and healed Naaman's leprosy (**see 2 Kings 5:1–14**). Each miracle was a demonstration of the living God, but perhaps his final, posthumous miracle—the raising of a dead man from his own grave—spoke loudest to the enduring nature of God's power.

This teaches us that a life surrendered to God leaves a spiritual inheritance that can impact others long after we are gone. You may not be a prophet like Elisha, but the faith, prayers, and seeds you sow in obedience to God's will remain active in the spirit long after your physical presence has faded.

> **"Blessed are the dead which die in the Lord from henceforth: Yea, saith the Spirit, that they may rest from their labours; and their works do follow them." – Revelation 14:13 (KJV)**

Death Cannot Intimidate the Power of God

The enemy thought that the death of the prophet would mean the end of his influence. But God showed that not even death could stop His purposes. The same God who raised Lazarus (**see John 11:43–44**) and Jesus (**see Matthew 28:5–6**) was at work in this tomb encounter.

This is a prophetic word to the church today: If the same Spirit that raised Jesus from the dead dwells in you, it will quicken—not only

19

your mortal body—but also every assignment, promise, and purpose God has spoken over your life (**see Romans 8:11**).

Even when situations look lifeless, even when the enemy believes he has buried your influence, God can breathe resurrection power into places everyone else has written off.

Personal Reflection

- What "dead places" in your life need the touch of God's resurrection power?

- Are you living in such a way that your spiritual influence will outlive you?

- Do you believe that the God who worked in Elisha's bones can work through you today?

Prayer of Activation

Lord, I thank You that Your anointing is not bound by time, death, or limitation. Let the same Spirit that was upon Elisha rest upon me—not for my glory, but for Yours. May my life be so yielded to You that long after I am gone, my works in the Spirit continue to impact lives. Revive every dead place in me and around me by Your power, in Jesus' name. Amen.

CHAPTER 2

ELISHA'S FINAL MIRACLE: LIFE FROM DEATH

Key Scripture

> "Then Elisha died, and they buried him. And the raiding bands from Moab invaded the land in the spring of the year. So it was, as they were burying a man, that suddenly they spied a band of raiders; and they put the man in the tomb of Elisha; and when the man was let down and touched the bones of Elisha, he revived and stood on his feet." – 2 Kings 13:20–21 (NKJV)

The Bible is filled with miracles, but few are as unique—or as mysterious—as this one. In most resurrection stories, the prophet or apostle is alive, speaking, or praying over the dead person. Elijah stretched himself over the widow's son three times and cried out to God (**see 1 Kings 17:21–22**). Jesus took the hand of Jairus' daughter and commanded her to rise (**see Mark 5:41–42**). Peter knelt down and prayed before telling Tabitha to get up (**see Acts 9:40**).

But in Elisha's final miracle, there was no prayer, no spoken word, no physical act of laying on hands—because Elisha was dead. The miracle came not from an action taken in that moment, but from the lingering presence of God's anointing resting on the prophet's bones.

Why Did This Happen After His Death?

This miracle was not random. God does nothing by accident. There are prophetic reasons why Elisha's last miracle occurred after his death:

1. To Prove the Endurance of God's Power

God's power is not confined to the lifespan of His servant. What He deposits in a life can still bear fruit beyond the grave.

> **"The grass withereth, the flower fadeth: but the word of our God shall stand for ever." – Isaiah 40:8 (KJV)**

2. To Testify to Israel in a Time of Spiritual Decline

The nation was drifting, enemies were invading, and faith was waning. God used this miracle to remind His people that He was still their Deliverer.

> **"Call unto me, and I will answer thee, and show thee great and mighty things, which thou knowest not." – Jeremiah 33:3 (KJV)**

3. To Demonstrate the Power of Legacy

Elisha's ministry had been about obedience, mentorship, and impartation. This miracle became his final act of impartation—raising another to life.

The Moabite Invasion: A Sudden Disruption

The resurrection was triggered by a moment of urgency and fear. While burying a man, the Israelites saw a Moabite raiding party approaching. These were not ceremonial priests performing a careful burial—they were men caught in crisis. They didn't have time to dig a new grave, perform rituals, or even mourn.

It was this sudden disruption that led them to throw the dead man into the tomb of Elisha. Sometimes, the greatest miracles happen in moments of chaos, when we are forced to abandon our plans and act in desperation.

> **"Be still, and know that I am God..." – Psalm 46:10 (KJV)**

In other words, the very crisis that threatened them became the doorway to a resurrection. The same can happen in your life—what looks like an interruption may be a divine setup for God's glory to be revealed.

Contact with the Bones

The text says the man "touched the bones of Elisha" and revived. The Hebrew word for "touched" here suggests not just a light brush, but a coming into contact or connection. This was not about the bones having mystical power—this was about the bones having been the vessel of God's Spirit.

The power was never in Elisha's humanity—it was in God's Spirit that had once saturated his life. And because God's presence had so permeated him during his ministry, even his bones carried a lingering impartation of life.

23

This aligns with the New Testament truth:

> **"...the anointing which ye have received of him abideth in you..." – 1 John 2:27 (KJV)**

Standing on His Feet

The moment the dead man touched Elisha's bones, he revived and stood on his feet. In scripture, standing is often symbolic of strength, restoration, and readiness.

- In Ezekiel's vision, when the breath of God entered the dry bones, they stood as a vast army (**see Ezekiel 37:10**).

- In **Acts 3:7–8**, when Peter lifted the lame man, immediately his feet and ankles were strengthened, and he stood, walking and leaping.

This shows us that God doesn't just revive you to lie there—He raises you so you can stand, move, and fulfill purpose again.

Lessons for Us Today

1. **God's Power Outlives His Servants** – The vessels change; the source remains.

2. **Your Anointing Leaves a Residue** – The way you live today will impact lives tomorrow.

3. **Desperate Situations Are Opportunities for Miracles** – Crisis moments are often the catalyst for resurrection power.

Personal Reflection

- Are you living in such a way that your walk with God will impact people beyond your lifetime?

- Do you recognize that even in seasons of crisis, God can bring forth resurrection?

- Are you cultivating an anointing that will outlast your name?

Prayer of Impartation

Father, I thank You for the example of Elisha's life. Teach me to live in such a way that Your Spirit saturates every part of me. Let my obedience, prayers, service, and faith leave a lasting impact. And in times of chaos, remind me that You are still able to bring life from death. I receive Your anointing, not just for my generation, but as a legacy for generations to come. In Jesus' name. Amen.

CHAPTER 3

THE ANOINTING'S ETERNAL SOURCE

Key Scripture

> "But it is the spirit in a person, the breath of the Almighty, that gives them understanding." – Job 32:8 (NIV)

The miracle of Elisha's bones teaches us a critical truth: the anointing does not originate in man. It flows from an eternal, inexhaustible Source: God Himself. This is why the anointing could remain in Elisha's bones long after his death. It was never "his" anointing in the sense of ownership—it was God's anointing upon him.

We must understand this if we are to walk in lasting spiritual influence. Too often, we think of the anointing as a personal possession—something we "have" or "carry" because of our own merit or spiritual discipline. But the anointing is on loan from the Eternal One, entrusted to us for His purposes.

The Source of All Anointing

From the beginning, scripture makes clear that God is the origin of all true power and anointing.

- In **Exodus 31:3,** God says of Bezalel: **"I have filled him with the Spirit of God, with wisdom, with understanding, with knowledge and with all kinds of skills." (NIV).**

- In **1 Samuel 16:13**, the Spirit of the Lord came mightily upon David after Samuel anointed him with oil.

- In **Isaiah 61:1**, the Messiah Himself declares: **"The Spirit of the Lord God is upon me; because the Lord hath anointed me…" (KJV).**

This makes it clear—anointing flows from the Spirit of the Lord, not from human effort alone.

Why the Source Matters

When you know the Source of your anointing, three things happen:

1. **You Walk in Humility** – You realize it's not your talent, charisma, or experience; it's God's enabling grace.

"Not that we are sufficient of ourselves to think any thing as of ourselves; but our sufficiency is of God." – 2 Corinthians 3:5 (KJV)

2. **You Avoid Burnout** – If God is the Source, then you don't have to manufacture results—you simply stay connected to Him.

"I am the vine, ye are the branches: He that abideth in me, and I in him, the same bringeth forth much fruit: for without me ye can do nothing." – John 15:5 (KJV)

3. **Your Impact Outlasts You** – Because the Source is eternal, the effect of the anointing can extend beyond your earthly life.

Why Elisha's Anointing Remained

Elisha's body died, but God's Spirit is eternal. The vessel perished, but the oil of God's presence had so thoroughly saturated him that it lingered—even in his bones.

Think about it: Elisha had spent his life as a man who not only received the double portion of Elijah's spirit (**see 2 Kings 2:9–15**) but also walked in consistent obedience to God. Every miracle he performed was the overflow of a relationship with the Eternal Source.

The anointing in his bones was like residual heat in a furnace—even after the fire is no longer visible, the warmth remains.

A Warning Against Imitation

There is a danger in thinking we can operate in the anointing apart from the Source. In **Acts 19:13–16**, the seven sons of Sceva tried to imitate Paul's authority by invoking the name of Jesus without truly knowing Him. The result was disastrous—they were overpowered and shamed.

This shows us that the anointing cannot be duplicated through human methods—it is imparted through divine relationship. Without connection to the Source, there is no lasting power.

Living in Continuous Connection

If we desire an anointing that not only impacts our lifetime but leaves a legacy, we must stay connected to God every single day. Prayer, worship, fasting, obedience, and intimacy with the Word keep the oil flowing.

> **"But my horn shalt thou exalt like the horn of an unicorn: I shall be anointed with fresh oil." – Psalm 92:10 (KJV)**

The "fresh oil" David spoke of represents the continual renewal of the Spirit's empowerment. You cannot live off yesterday's anointing. Elisha's bones performed one final miracle, but in his lifetime, he sought God daily for fresh empowerment.

Personal Reflection

- Do you recognize God as the sole Source of the anointing on your life?

- Are you seeking daily renewal, or are you trying to live off past experiences with God?

- Is your ministry, service, or calling fueled by your own effort or by the overflow of His presence?

Prayer for Fresh Oil

Lord, I acknowledge You as the Source of every gift, every ability, and every anointing on my life. Forgive me for the times I have tried to operate in my own strength. Keep me connected to You—the true Vine—so that I may bear lasting fruit. Saturate me afresh today with

Your Spirit, and let my life carry the fragrance of Your presence for generations to come. In Jesus' name. Amen.

PART II

LESSONS FROM THE BONES

PART II

LESSONS FROM THE BONES

CHAPTER 4

DEAD YET SPEAKING

Key Scripture

> **"By faith Abel offered unto God a more excellent sacrifice than Cain, by which he obtained witness that he was righteous, God testifying of his gifts: and by it he being dead yet speaketh." – Hebrews 11:4 (KJV)**

The Bible tells us that Abel, though long dead, still "speaks." His testimony of faith and obedience continues to echo across the pages of history. In the same way, Elisha—though dead—was still "speaking" on the day a lifeless man touched his bones and came alive.

God used this posthumous miracle as more than an act of power; it was a prophetic declaration: *A life surrendered to God will continue to bear witness even after the vessel is gone.*

This is the kind of legacy every believer should long for—not simply to be remembered for what we did, but to leave a spiritual imprint that continues to influence and transform lives long after we have gone to be with the Lord.

A Voice Beyond the Grave

Elisha had no opportunity to prepare for this miracle. He didn't orchestrate it; he wasn't there to speak words of healing. Yet, his life was so saturated with the Spirit of God that even in silence and stillness—yes, even in death—his testimony spoke.

It declared:

- God's power is not bound by time.
- God's purposes will outlive the vessel.
- God's Word will not return void **(see Isaiah 55:11)**.

When the dead man revived, the living witnesses could not deny it—God's anointing was still present.

The Power of a Godly Legacy

A godly life sends ripples through generations. Your acts of obedience, your prayers, your sacrifices—they don't just vanish when you do. They continue to "speak" in the spiritual realm.

David's worship still speaks today through the Psalms. Paul's letters still speak across the centuries. The faith of countless unnamed saints continues to shape the lives of their children and grandchildren.

> **"The memory of the just is blessed..." – Proverbs 10:7 (KJV)**

The question we must ask ourselves is: *What will my life speak when I am gone?* Will it testify of faithfulness, love, integrity, and Spirit-led obedience? Or will it leave no lasting witness at all?

Your Life as a Living Epistle

Paul tells the believers in Corinth:

> **"Ye are our epistle written in our hearts, known and read of all men." – 2 Corinthians 3:2 (KJV)**

This means people are reading your life right now—whether you realize it or not. Every choice you make, every act of kindness, every stand for truth—it's all leaving an imprint on the lives of those who come after you.

Elisha's "last sermon" was not preached with words; it was demonstrated through resurrection power. And for those present, that moment became a life-altering testimony.

Dead to Self, Alive to God

While Elisha was physically dead, we must also consider the principle of being spiritually "dead" to self while still living. Paul writes:

> **"I am crucified with Christ: nevertheless I live; yet not I, but Christ liveth in me..." – Galatians 2:20 (KJV)**

When you die to your own will, ambitions, and pride, and live fully for God, your life becomes a pure channel of His power. That's the kind of vessel God can so saturate that even in your absence, the residue of His presence remains.

Prayers That Outlive You

One of the ways your life can "speak" beyond your years is through prayer. The prayers you pray today are seeds that can bear fruit long after you are gone. Many of us are living in the answers to prayers prayed by parents, grandparents, pastors, and intercessors who are now in glory.

"The effectual fervent prayer of a righteous man availeth much." – James 5:16 (KJV)

Like incense that lingers in a room after the source is gone, your prayers leave a fragrance in the spiritual atmosphere.

Personal Reflection

- What message will your life speak when you are no longer here?

- Are you sowing seeds today that will bless people you may never meet?

- Have you allowed God to saturate you so deeply that His presence can work through your legacy?

Prayer for a Speaking Legacy

Lord, I want my life to be a testimony that continues to speak even when my voice is silent. Let my choices, words, actions, and faith leave a godly imprint for generations to come. Saturate me with Your Spirit until every part of me is marked by Your presence. And when my earthly journey is over, let my legacy still point people to You. In Jesus' name. Amen.

CHAPTER 5

YOUR ANOINTING IS NOT TIME-LIMITED

Key Scripture

> "For the gifts and calling of God are without repentance." – Romans 11:29 (KJV)

The world measures effectiveness by time. We are told there's a "season" for success, a "prime" for productivity, and an "expiration date" for influence. But in the kingdom of God, the anointing is not time-limited. When God calls and anoints a person, His empowerment is not revoked simply because years have passed, the vessel has aged, or circumstances have changed.

This was the truth on display in the tomb of Elisha. His ministry on earth had ended years earlier. His physical body had returned to dust, yet the power of God that had once rested upon him was still active—still capable of bringing the dead to life.

Elisha's posthumous miracle is a bold statement to every believer: *What God deposits in you will outlast seasons, situations, and even your own lifetime.*

The Permanence of God's Calling

Paul's statement in **Romans 11:29** was written in the context of God's covenant with Israel, but it reveals a universal truth—God's gifts and calling are irrevocable. He does not call you one day and change His mind the next.

- Moses thought his time was over after forty years in the wilderness, yet God called him at eighty to deliver Israel (**see Exodus 3:10**).

- Caleb was eighty-five when he declared, "Give me this mountain" (**see Joshua 14:10–12**).

- Anna, the prophetess, was well advanced in years, yet she still served in the temple day and night and was among the first to recognize Jesus as the Messiah (**see Luke 2:36–38**).

These examples show that the anointing doesn't expire with age—it remains as long as God has a purpose for you to fulfill.

Breaking the Lie of "Too Late"

The enemy loves to whisper, *"You've missed your window. You're too old, too far gone, too broken. It's over."* But the Word of God dismantles that lie.

Consider Sarah. By the time she conceived Isaac, she was well past childbearing years, yet God's promise stood firm (**see Genesis 21:1–2**). Consider Paul, who spent years persecuting the church before becoming one of its greatest apostles (**see Acts 9:1–20**). God doesn't measure your usefulness by the clock—He measures it by your willingness to obey Him now.

> **"Being confident of this very thing, that He which hath begun a good work in you will perform it until the day of Jesus Christ." – Philippians 1:6 (KJV)**

The Anointing Is for Purpose, Not Popularity

The anointing is not seasonal like a trend—it is purposeful. It remains active because the mission God gave you is still relevant. Elisha's anointing was for the work of God in Israel, and that purpose did not vanish because the prophet died.

When the dead man touched Elisha's bones, it wasn't about Elisha's fame—it was about God's agenda. This miracle was a divine reminder to Israel that the same God who moved in the past was still moving in the present.

Stewarding the Anointing Over Time

While the anointing itself is not time-limited, your stewardship of it matters. The oil flows most freely through a life kept in alignment with God's will. If you allow bitterness, compromise, or pride to take root, you may not lose the anointing, but you can hinder its flow through you.

"Quench not the Spirit." – 1 Thessalonians 5:19 (KJV)

Elisha kept himself in a posture of obedience and faithfulness throughout his life, which is why the residue of God's power remained even in his bones.

A Legacy That Outruns the Clock

If you are walking in God's will, you can rest assured that your best years are not behind you—your anointing is still active. And when your earthly work is done, the seeds you've sown and the prayers you've prayed will keep producing fruit.

The kingdom of God measures time differently. God can bring a harvest decades after a seed is sown. He can cause a prayer you prayed twenty years ago to be answered today. And just as with Elisha, He can release miracles through the residue of what He once placed in your life.

Personal Reflection

- Have you believed the lie that your time of usefulness in God's kingdom has passed?

- Are you stewarding the anointing on your life with faithfulness and humility?

- Do you recognize that God's purpose for you is still active, regardless of your age or season?

Prayer to Embrace the Timeless Anointing

Father, thank You that the gifts and calling You've placed on my life are without expiration. Forgive me for believing the lie that my best days are behind me. Help me to steward the anointing with humility, faith, and obedience. Let my life bear fruit in every season, and may my legacy continue to bring You glory long after I am gone. In Jesus' name. Amen.

CHAPTER 6

GOD'S TIMING AND UNLIKELY MOMENTS

Key Scripture

"To every thing there is a season, and a time to every purpose under the heaven." – Ecclesiastes 3:1 (KJV)

God is not bound by our calendars, clocks, or comfort zones. He chooses His moments with precision, and He often releases His greatest works in the most unlikely situations. The miracle of Elisha's bones was one such moment.

This was not a carefully planned, reverent resurrection service. It was not preceded by worship music, fasting, or hours of intercessory prayer. It happened in the middle of chaos—during a hurried burial, under the threat of an enemy raid. In other words, the miracle occurred in a moment nobody expected and in a setting nobody would have chosen.

And yet, this is often God's way. He specializes in showing up when it seems least likely and using circumstances we would never pick to display His glory.

The Scene: Chaos at the Graveside

Imagine it. Friends and family are gathered to bury a loved one. Mourners are weeping. The body is ready for final rest. Then suddenly, someone shouts in panic: "Moabite raiders!"

The air shifts instantly from grief to survival. In desperation, they abandon the careful burial process, grabbing the body and placing it in the nearest available tomb—Elisha's. No one was thinking about miracles in that moment. Their focus was escape.

And then, it happened. The dead man touched Elisha's bones. Life surged through him. He stood to his feet.

God's Unlikely Timing

This miracle reminds us that God is not limited to what we think are "spiritual moments." He doesn't need a set stage to move. He can turn an interruption into an opportunity.

- Moses was tending sheep—an ordinary day—when God called from the burning bush (**see Exodus 3:1–4**).

- Gideon was threshing wheat in hiding when the angel appeared and declared him a mighty warrior (**see Judges 6:11–12**).

- Peter was cleaning his fishing nets when Jesus called him to follow (**see Luke 5:2–10**).

The timing seemed random, but God's plan was deliberate.

Why God Uses Unlikely Moments

1. To Prove It's All Him

When the setting is ordinary or chaotic, no one can claim the glory for the outcome.

"That your faith should not stand in the wisdom of men, but in the power of God." – 1 Corinthians 2:5 (KJV)

2. To Strengthen Faith in Hard Times

God often chooses dark seasons to release light, so that hope is restored when it's most needed.

3. To Interrupt the Enemy's Plans

The Moabite raiders expected to cause fear and disruption; instead, their intrusion became the setting for a resurrection.

When God's Moment Arrives

The miracle at Elisha's tomb didn't require a sermon, a strategy, or a schedule—it only required God's timing.

There's a deep encouragement here: *When it's God's moment, nothing can stop it—not fear, not enemy attack, not human limitation.*

Joseph went from the prison to the palace in a single day because Pharaoh had a dream that required his interpretation (**see Genesis 41:14**). The woman with the issue of blood was healed instantly when she touched Jesus' garment (**see Mark 5:25–34**). Paul and Silas were released from prison at midnight because an earthquake shook the foundations (**see Acts 16:25–26**).

God's timing may feel "late" to us, but it is always right on schedule.

Trusting God in the Unexpected

Sometimes, we resist the unexpected because it disrupts our plans. But the miracle of Elisha's bones reminds us that God's interruptions are often divine appointments in disguise. What feels like chaos to us may be the perfect stage for His glory.

"My times are in thy hand..." – Psalm 31:15 (KJV)

Personal Reflection

- Have you been frustrated by God's timing because it didn't match your expectations?

- Do you recognize that God can move in your life, even in chaotic or inconvenient moments?

- Are you willing to embrace divine interruptions as opportunities for His power to be revealed?

Prayer for Trust in God's Timing

Lord, I surrender my schedule to You. I acknowledge that my times are in Your hands. Help me to trust that even the unexpected moments are part of Your perfect plan. Open my eyes to see divine opportunities hidden in what looks like chaos. Let me be ready for Your move—anytime, anywhere. In Jesus' name. Amen.

PART III

WALKING IN AN ANOINTING THAT OUTLASTS YOU

CHAPTER 7

BUILDING A LIFE WORTH REMEMBERING

Key Scripture

"The memory of the just is blessed: but the name of the wicked shall rot." – Proverbs 10:7 (KJV)

When the nameless man's body touched the bones of Elisha and came alive, it wasn't just a resurrection—it was the echo of a life well-lived. Elisha's ministry had been marked by faithfulness, obedience, and power. He left behind more than memories; he left behind a spiritual deposit that could still bring life to others.

The truth is, every one of us is building a legacy right now. Whether we realize it or not, our daily choices, attitudes, and actions are creating a spiritual "trail" for others to follow. The question is: *What kind of life will you leave behind when your time on earth is over?*

A life worth remembering is not measured by the applause of people, the size of our bank account, or the titles we accumulate—it's measured by the depth of our relationship with God and the eternal impact we have on others.

A Life Anchored in God's Presence

Elisha's ministry began when he left everything to follow Elijah (**see 1 Kings 19:19–21**). From that moment on, he pursued God's presence above all else. He sought a double portion of Elijah's spirit—not for fame, but for effectiveness in God's work (**see 2 Kings 2:9**).

To build a life worth remembering, we must be anchored in God's presence, refusing to be swayed by worldly distractions.

> **"One thing have I desired of the Lord, that will I seek after; that I may dwell in the house of the Lord all the days of my life..." – Psalm 27:4 (KJV)**

A Life Marked by Obedience

Faith without obedience is hollow. Elisha's miracles flowed from a life of consistent obedience—whether it was instructing Naaman to dip seven times in the Jordan (**see 2 Kings 5:10**) or multiplying a widow's oil (**see 2 Kings 4:1–7**).

When you obey God—even in the small things—you're laying down stones of remembrance that will outlast you.

> **"If ye be willing and obedient, ye shall eat the good of the land." – Isaiah 1:19 (KJV)**

A Life That Serves Others

Elisha's ministry was not self-centered; it was about meeting needs. He healed, provided, prophesied, and even intervened in national matters for the good of others.

A life worth remembering is one that pours into others—not just for personal recognition, but because love compels us.

"For even the Son of man came not to be ministered unto, but to minister, and to give his life a ransom for many." – Mark 10:45 (KJV)

A Life That Leaves a Spiritual Deposit

The miracle in the tomb was possible because Elisha had allowed God to saturate his life so deeply that even his bones carried the residue of the anointing.

When you live in continual surrender to the Spirit, your prayers, worship, and service leave a deposit that can bless people you will never meet.

"...their works do follow them." – Revelation 14:13 (KJV)

Practical Ways to Build a Life Worth Remembering

- **Stay rooted in the Word** – It's the only foundation that will endure (**see Matthew 7:24–25**).

- **Invest in people** – Mentor, disciple, and encourage those God brings into your life (**see 2 Timothy 2:2**).

- **Pray without ceasing** – Let prayer be the atmosphere of your life (**see 1 Thessalonians 5:17**).

- **Live with eternity in view** – Make decisions that will matter in the light of forever (**see Colossians 3:2**).

The Danger of Living for Self

The opposite of a life worth remembering is a life lived for self. The rich man in **Luke 16:19–31** lived in luxury but left no eternal impact. When he died, he had no spiritual legacy—only regret.

Your life is either sowing seeds for the kingdom or scattering to the wind. The choice is yours.

Personal Reflection

- If you died today, what would your life "speak" to others?

- Are you investing your time and resources into things that will outlast you?

- What intentional steps are you taking to leave a spiritual inheritance?

Prayer for a Life That Lasts

Lord, I don't want to live for myself. I want my life to be worth remembering—not for my glory, but for Yours. Teach me to stay rooted in Your presence, to walk in obedience, and to serve others with love. Let me leave a spiritual deposit that will bless generations after me. In Jesus' name. Amen.

CHAPTER 8

WHAT YOU LEAVE BEHIND MATTERS

Key Scripture

> **"A good man leaveth an inheritance to his children's children: and the wealth of the sinner is laid up for the just." – Proverbs 13:22 (KJV)**

Every person leaves something behind when they depart this life. For some, it's a memory; for others, it's a legacy. The question is not if you will leave something, but what you will leave.

Elisha's life shows us that what you deposit in the Spirit can outlive you. His anointing was so deeply woven into his being that years after his death, it was still capable of bringing a dead man back to life. That's not just history—it's a prophetic message: the spiritual inheritance you leave is more valuable than any material possession.

More Than Material Wealth

When **Proverbs 13:22** speaks of a "good man" leaving an inheritance, it is not limited to finances or property. Material things are temporary; they can be spent, lost, or destroyed. But a spiritual inheritance is eternal—it continues to shape lives, guide decisions, and release blessings for generations.

Abraham left behind more than flocks and land; he left a covenant with God that still blesses the descendants of faith today (**see Genesis 12:1–3**). David left Solomon not just a throne, but blueprints for the temple and a heart after God. Paul left Timothy not wealth, but a charge to guard the gospel (**see 2 Timothy 1:13–14**).

The Weight of Spiritual Deposits

Your prayer life, your faith, your obedience, your testimony—these are deposits that outlast your years. Every prayer you pray over your children, every word of encouragement you speak to a struggling believer, every seed you sow into the kingdom is a piece of your spiritual inheritance.

> **"...their works do follow them." – Revelation 14:13 (KJV)**

When you live yielded to the Spirit, you are building an inheritance that no thief can steal and no moth can destroy (**see Matthew 6:19–20**).

The Two Kinds of Inheritance

1. **Flesh-Born Inheritance** – Things accumulated in your own strength—money, possessions, personal achievements. These have value but are temporary.

2. **Spirit-Born Inheritance** – Things birthed by God's Spirit in your life—faith, wisdom, godly example, prayer covering, kingdom investments. These are eternal and cannot decay.

Elisha's inheritance was Spirit-born, which is why it still had power long after his flesh had returned to the dust.

Passing the Mantle

A spiritual inheritance is not automatic—it must be passed intentionally. Elijah passed his mantle to Elisha (**see 2 Kings 2:13–14**), and Elisha could have done the same for another if there had been a willing and prepared successor.

In our generation, passing the mantle means:

- Mentoring those younger in the faith.
- Teaching biblical truth without compromise.
- Modeling a life of prayer, holiness, and service.
- Empowering others to walk in their calling.

What Happens If You Leave Nothing?

The danger of neglecting to leave a spiritual inheritance is that the next generation starts from scratch—or worse, starts at a deficit. Judges 2:10 gives a sobering example: after Joshua's generation died, **"there arose another generation after them, which knew not the Lord, nor yet the works which he had done for Israel."**

This happened because the testimony of God's works was not intentionally preserved and passed down.

Building Your Inheritance Now

Here are some ways you can start building a spiritual inheritance today:

- Pray for your family daily, even if they don't follow Christ yet.
- Keep a journal of God's faithfulness and answered prayers to pass down.
- Speak blessings over your children, grandchildren, or spiritual sons and daughters.
- Invest in kingdom work that will continue after you are gone.

Personal Reflection

- Are you intentionally building a spiritual inheritance, or are you only focused on material provision?

- Who are you mentoring or discipling that could carry the mantle forward?

- If you left this world today, what spiritual deposit would remain?

Prayer for a Lasting Inheritance

Lord, help me to live in such a way that I leave behind more than possessions—I want to leave a legacy of faith, obedience, and love for You. Show me who to invest in, mentor, and encourage. Let my life sow seeds that will bear fruit for generations to come, and may my spiritual inheritance bring glory to Your name forever. In Jesus' name. Amen.

CHAPTER 9

WHEN THE ANOINTING MEETS THE IMPOSSIBLE

Key Scripture

"Behold, I am the Lord, the God of all flesh: is there any thing too hard for me?" – Jeremiah 32:27 (KJV)

Some moments in life seem completely beyond hope—dead ends, broken dreams, irreversible losses. In the natural, they look like the end of the road. But when the anointing of God collides with the impossible, the end becomes the beginning, the grave becomes the birthplace, and what was once dead stands to life again.

The miracle of Elisha's bones is a picture of this reality. A dead man—past all medical help, beyond all human ability—was suddenly revived by contact with the residue of God's anointing. This was not a gradual improvement; it was an instant transformation.

It was a prophetic declaration to Israel and to us: When God's anointing enters a situation, impossibility is no longer the final word.

God's Specialty: The Impossible

From Genesis to Revelation, scripture shows us that God is not intimidated by what seems humanly hopeless.

- Abraham and Sarah had a child long after their bodies were past the natural ability to conceive (**see Genesis 18:10–14**).

- Moses parted the Red Sea with nothing but a staff and God's command (**see Exodus 14:21–22**).

- Joshua saw the walls of Jericho crumble without a single weapon—just obedience and a shout (**see Joshua 6:20**).

- Jesus fed thousands with five loaves and two fish (**see Matthew 14:17–21**).

- Lazarus walked out of the tomb after four days (**see John 11:43–44**).

In every case, the impossible yielded to the anointing.

The Nature of the Anointing

The anointing is God's power flowing through a willing vessel to accomplish what only He can do. It is not limited to preaching or church services—it is God's empowerment in any sphere of life. It is the divine enablement to do what cannot be done without Him.

This is why, even though Elisha's body was lifeless, the Spirit's deposit in his bones could still accomplish God's work. The anointing is not bound by circumstance, location, or even time.

When the Anointing Confronts Death

In **2 Kings 13:21**, the dead man was on his way to a final resting place when he encountered the bones of Elisha. In that moment, the Spirit of God reversed the irreversible. This shows us that:

1. The anointing is stronger than death.

"O death, where is thy sting? O grave, where is thy victory?" – *1 Corinthians 15:55 (KJV).*

2. God can turn interruptions into miracles.

The Moabite raid that disrupted the burial was the very thing that positioned the man for resurrection.

3. One touch is enough.

The man didn't need a sermon, oil, or laying on of hands. He just needed contact with the anointing.

Your Impossible Situation Is God's Opportunity

Sometimes God allows you to face the impossible so that only His power can receive the glory. When Gideon faced the Midianite army with only 300 men (**see Judges 7**), it was so Israel would know their victory came from the Lord alone.

The same is true in your life:

- That financial need is a stage for His provision.
- That broken relationship is a canvas for His restoration.
- That diagnosis is an opportunity for His healing.

Barriers to Believing the Impossible

Before God moves in the impossible, He often deals with the barriers in our faith:

1. **Fear** – Like the disciples in the storm (**see Mark 4:40**), we let fear drown out faith.

2. **Logic** – We try to reason how God will do it, forgetting His ways are higher (**see Isaiah 55:8–9**).

3. **Past Disappointment** – We hesitate to believe again because we've been let down before.

But the anointing bypasses human limitation. It doesn't ask, *"Can this be done?"* It declares, *"It is done."*

Positioning Yourself for the Anointing to Work

Even though the dead man in **2 Kings 13:21** had no choice in the matter, we as the living can intentionally position ourselves for the anointing to meet our impossibilities:

- **Stay close to God's presence** – Miracles happen where His glory dwells (**see Psalm 16:11**).

- **Walk in obedience** – The anointing flows where God's will is honored (**see Deuteronomy 28:1–2**).

- **Surround yourself with the right atmosphere** – Faith grows when you are around those who believe God can move (**see Mark 2:1–5**).

Personal Reflection

- Are you allowing fear, logic, or disappointment to limit your expectation of God?

- What "dead" situations in your life need to come into contact with the anointing?

- Do you truly believe that nothing is too hard for the Lord?

Prayer for Faith in the Impossible

Father, I thank You that nothing is too hard for You. Forgive me for limiting You by my fears, reasoning, or past disappointments. Today, I bring every impossible situation into Your presence. Let Your anointing meet it, break its power, and release resurrection life. I trust You to do what no man can do, in Jesus' name. Amen.

PART IV

PROPHETIC IMPLICATIONS FOR THE CHURCH TODAY

CHAPTER 10

THE SLEEPING CHURCH AND THE POWER OF AWAKENING

Key Scripture

> **"Wherefore he saith, Awake thou that sleepest, and arise from the dead, and Christ shall give thee light." – Ephesians 5:14 (KJV)**

The miracle of Elisha's bones is not just a fascinating piece of Old Testament history—it is a prophetic picture of what God wants to do in His church today. Just as the dead man came to life when he touched the prophet's bones, God desires to awaken His sleeping church with a fresh encounter of His resurrection power.

We are living in a time when much of the body of Christ is spiritually drowsy. The music may be loud, the programs may be polished, the buildings may be full—but in many places, the spiritual pulse is faint. We have the appearance of life without the force of the Spirit's power flowing through us.

And yet, just as in Elisha's day, God is still able to revive in an instant when His people come into contact with the residue of His true anointing.

A Church in Need of Awakening

The sleeping church is not always aware of her own slumber. In **Revelation 3:1–2**, Jesus says to the church in Sardis:

> **"I know thy works, that thou hast a name that thou livest, and art dead. Be watchful, and strengthen the things which remain, that are ready to die…" (KJV)**

Sardis had a reputation for being alive, but in reality, it was spiritually lifeless. This is the danger when the church becomes content with activity instead of anointing, busyness instead of breakthrough, numbers instead of discipleship.

A sleeping church can:

- Lose her prophetic voice in the culture.
- Forget her mission to win the lost.
- Settle for programs instead of presence.

God's Pattern for Awakening

Whenever God awakens His people, it often happens in moments of crisis—when we are jolted into realizing how far we have drifted. The burial in **2 Kings 13:21** was interrupted by an enemy attack, but that disruption led to resurrection.

Likewise, God often allows disruption to awaken His church. Persecution, cultural shaking, or even the exposure of sin can be His mercy at work—shaking us so that we will return to Him wholeheartedly.

> **"It is time to seek the Lord, till he come and rain righteousness upon you." – Hosea 10:12 (KJV)**

From Complacency to Contact

The man in Elisha's tomb did not come back to life until he made contact with the prophet's bones. In the same way, the church will not awaken until she makes contact with the real presence of God again. Not just sermons about Him, not just songs about Him, but a direct encounter with Him.

This contact happens when:

- We return to the altar in repentance (**see Joel 2:12–13**).
- We hunger for His presence more than human approval (**see Psalm 42:1–2**).
- We yield fully to the Holy Spirit's leading (**see Acts 4:31**).

Signs of a Church Being Awakened

When the Spirit begins to awaken a sleeping church, certain signs follow:

1. **Renewed Conviction** – Sin is no longer tolerated but confessed and forsaken (**see 1 John 1:9**).

2. **Fervent Prayer** – Intercession becomes the heartbeat of the congregation (**see Acts 1:14**).

3. **Bold Evangelism** – Believers speak openly about Christ without fear (**see Acts 4:20**).

4. **Supernatural Manifestations** – Healing, deliverance, and prophetic utterance flow freely (**see Mark 16:17–18**).

5. **Radical Generosity** – Resources are shared to meet needs and advance the kingdom (**see Acts 4:32–35**).

The Danger of Refusing to Awaken

A church that refuses to awaken is like the five foolish virgins in **Matthew 25:1–13**—caught unprepared when the Bridegroom arrives. They had lamps but no oil. In other words, they had form without power, appearance without anointing.

The result was tragic—they missed their moment.

A Call to the Church Today

The miracle in Elisha's tomb shouts to us: *If God can cause a dead man to rise from contact with dry bones, He can cause His church to rise from spiritual death.*

This is the hour for leaders, intercessors, and everyday believers to cry out for an awakening that will shake us out of comfort and into kingdom assignment.

> **"Wilt thou not revive us again: that thy people may rejoice in thee?" – Psalm 85:6 (KJV)**

Personal Reflection

- Are you spiritually awake, or have you drifted into complacency?

- Is your church pursuing God's presence above all else, or are you content with programs?

- What steps can you take personally to press into a fresh encounter with the Lord?

Prayer for Awakening

Lord, awaken Your church. Shake us from our complacency and cause us to burn again with holy fire. Remove our reliance on human effort and draw us back to Your presence. Let revival begin in me, and let it spread through my church, my city, and my nation. We refuse to settle for a name that we are alive while being dead—breathe on us again, in Jesus' name. Amen.

CHAPTER 11

ANOINTING FOR GENERATIONAL REVIVAL

Key Scripture

> "One generation shall praise thy works to another, and shall declare thy mighty acts." – Psalm 145:4 (KJV)

The miracle of Elisha's bones was not simply for the benefit of one dead man—it was a prophetic demonstration for the next generation. Long after Elisha's voice was silent, his life still spoke. Long after his ministry had concluded, the anointing he carried still released life.

This is the nature of true revival—it is not confined to a single moment, a single leader, or a single generation. When God releases His power, it is meant to flow forward, igniting faith in those who come after us.

If the church is going to experience lasting revival, it must be a generational revival—one that burns in our hearts today and still burns in our children and grandchildren tomorrow.

The Pattern of Generational Fire

Throughout scripture, God's plan has always been to pass the flame from one generation to the next:

- Abraham → Isaac → Jacob – The covenant promise was renewed through each generation (**see Genesis 17:7**).

- Moses → Joshua – Moses laid hands on Joshua, imparting wisdom and leadership (**see Deuteronomy 34:9**).

- Elijah → Elisha – The prophetic mantle was passed to continue the work (**see 2 Kings 2:13–14**).

- Paul → Timothy – Paul urged Timothy to "stir up the gift" that was in him through impartation (**see 2 Timothy 1:6**).

But notice this: in each case, the fire did not pass automatically. It was intentionally transferred through teaching, mentorship, and demonstration of God's power.

Why Revival Often Dies Out

Many revivals throughout history burned brightly for a season but faded within a generation because the fire was not intentionally passed down. The reason is not that God's power weakened—it's that the next generation was never fully discipled to carry it.

Judges 2:10 offers one of the most sobering warnings in the Bible:

> **"And also all that generation were gathered unto their fathers: and there arose another generation after them, which knew not the Lord, nor yet the works which he had done for Israel." (KJV).**

In other words, the miraculous works of God were not adequately communicated, celebrated, or imparted. The result? Spiritual amnesia.

Impartation Requires Intention

If we want an anointing that will still speak when we are gone, we must be deliberate about impartation. This means:

1. **Mentoring the Next Generation** – Invest in teaching, praying for, and walking alongside younger believers.

2. **Modeling a Life of Power and Purity** – Let them see the anointing in action through your obedience.

3. **Making Room for Them to Minister** – Allow younger leaders to step into their calling while you are still here to guide them.

4. **Telling the Stories of God's Works** – Keep testimonies alive so faith is sparked in those who hear (**see Psalm 78:4**).

The Role of the Older and the Younger

Generational revival requires both the older generation and the younger generation to honor one another.

- The older must not despise the zeal of the young, but guide it.
- The younger must not dismiss the wisdom of the seasoned, but receive it.

This mutual honor ensures that the anointing doesn't die with one group but flows like a river from age to age.

> **"And also upon the servants and upon the handmaids in those days will I pour out my spirit." – Joel 2:29 (KJV)**

Elisha's Bones as a Generational Prophecy

The miracle in Elisha's tomb is a living prophecy: *What God deposits in you can raise up someone you will never meet.* The dead man who was revived may have gone on to tell his children and grandchildren about the God of Israel, sparking faith in future generations.

This is what happens when you leave behind more than possessions—you leave behind power, testimony, and spiritual inheritance.

Practical Steps to Leave a Generational Anointing

- **Pray for Your Family Daily** – Cover your children, grandchildren, and spiritual sons and daughters in intercession.

- **Write Down Your Testimonies** – Keep a written record of God's faithfulness for future generations to read.

- **Live Transparently Before Them** – Let them see your victories and how you overcome challenges through faith.

- **Release the Mantle Before You Go** – Don't take your gifts and wisdom to the grave—pass them on while you have time.

Personal Reflection

- Are you intentionally preparing the next generation to walk in God's power?

- Have you made room for younger believers to serve and grow in ministry?

- What spiritual inheritance will your children—or those you disciple—receive from you?

Prayer for Generational Revival

Lord, let my life be a bridge for Your power to flow to the next generation. Keep me from holding on to what You have given me out of fear or pride. Show me who to mentor, who to pour into, and who to release into their calling. Let the anointing You have placed on my life ignite revival in my children's children until Jesus returns. In His name I pray. Amen.

CHAPTER 12

GRAVEYARD MIRACLES IN THE LAST DAYS

Key Scripture

> **"Thus saith the Lord God unto these bones; Behold, I will cause breath to enter into you, and ye shall live." – Ezekiel 37:5 (KJV)**

The miracle in Elisha's tomb is more than a historical account—it is a prophetic shadow of what God desires to do in the last days. Just as a dead man was revived by touching the bones of a prophet, the Spirit of God is poised to bring resurrection life to people, churches, and nations that the world has already declared spiritually dead.

We are living in a generation that often celebrates spiritual decay, where faith is mocked, sin is normalized, and truth is redefined. Many look at the spiritual landscape and see only a graveyard—a place of what used to be alive but is now cold and lifeless. But graveyards are not a problem for the God who raises the dead. In fact, they are the perfect setting for Him to display His glory.

Prophetic Picture: Ezekiel's Valley of Dry Bones

Ezekiel 37 offers one of the clearest parallels to Elisha's bones. The prophet is taken by the Spirit into a valley filled with dry bones—lifeless, scattered, and without hope. God asks him:

"Son of man, can these bones live?" – Ezekiel 37:3 (KJV)

In the natural, the answer was obvious: No. Bones don't come back to life. But God tells Ezekiel to prophesy to the bones, and as he does, the bones come together, flesh covers them, and breath enters them until they stand as a great army.

This is the heartbeat of the Elisha's bones miracle—God breathing life into what man has given up on.

Graveyards in Our Time

A "graveyard" doesn't always mean a literal burial place. Spiritually speaking, a graveyard can be:

- A church that once burned with revival fire but is now cold and formal.

- A believer who once walked closely with God but is now bound in sin or apathy.

- A community that has been given over to darkness, violence, and unbelief.

- A calling or dream that was once vibrant but now feels buried by disappointment.

These are the places God is targeting in the last days—not to condemn them, but to resurrect them.

The Nature of Last-Day Resurrection Power

In the end times, revival will not be about hype, lights, or personalities—it will be about raw encounters with God's resurrection power. Just as the dead man didn't get up because of human effort, the last-day move of God will be marked by the undeniable truth that only God could have done this.

- Dead churches will come alive.
- Hardened sinners will be radically transformed overnight.
- Entire communities will be turned upside down by the gospel.

> **"For the earth shall be filled with the knowledge of the glory of the Lord, as the waters cover the sea." – Habakkuk 2:14 (KJV)**

Why God Waits Until It Looks Hopeless

It is not uncommon for God to wait until a situation appears utterly hopeless before He moves. Lazarus was dead four days before Jesus arrived (**see John 11:39–44**). Abraham and Sarah's bodies were "as good as dead" before Isaac was conceived (**see Romans 4:19–21**). The Red Sea did not part until Pharaoh's army was closing in (**see Exodus 14:21–22**).

God often does this so there will be no confusion about who gets the glory. In the same way, the end-time outpouring will come in a season when it seems least likely—when the moral decline is steepest, when faith seems weakest, when darkness appears strongest.

The Church as God's Last-Day Elisha

In a prophetic sense, the church is called to be like Elisha's bones in the last days—a carrier of resurrection life. Even if the world sees us as "buried" under persecution, irrelevance, or ridicule, the anointing within us can still bring life to the spiritually dead when they come in contact with the true gospel.

This means we cannot afford to dilute our message or hide our light. We must be ready for God to use us at any moment, even in places and times we do not expect.

> **"Arise, shine; for thy light is come, and the glory of the Lord is risen upon thee." – Isaiah 60:1 (KJV)**

What Graveyard Miracles Will Require from Us

1. **A People Saturated in God's Presence** – Like Elisha, we must walk so closely with God that His power remains evident in our lives.

2. **A Bold Prophetic Voice** – We must speak life where others speak death, declaring God's Word over impossible situations.

3. **A Refusal to Give Up on the "Dead"** – We must see with God's eyes and believe for resurrection where others see only ruin.

The Final Harvest

Jesus said, **"The harvest truly is plenteous, but the labourers are few" (Matthew 9:37 - KJV).** The graveyard miracles of the last days will be part of the final harvest before His return. Entire regions will be swept into the kingdom. The prodigals will come home. Those who were once enemies of the gospel will become its boldest preachers.

And just as in Elisha's tomb, these resurrections will not come through elaborate human effort—they will come through supernatural encounters with the living God.

Personal Reflection

- Where do you see "graveyards" in your life, church, or community?

- Do you believe God can still breathe life into what seems beyond hope?

- Are you willing to be a carrier of resurrection life to those the world has written off?

Prayer for Last-Day Resurrection Power

Lord, I thank You that no grave is too deep, no situation too hopeless, and no heart too hard for Your power. I ask You to breathe life into the places that have been declared dead—in my life, in my church, in my city, and in the nations. Use me as a carrier of Your anointing in these last days, that many may come alive in Christ before Your return. In Jesus' name. Amen.

CONCLUSION

ANOINTED UNTIL THE END...AND BEYOND

Key Scripture

> "I have fought a good fight, I have finished my course, I have kept the faith: Henceforth there is laid up for me a crown of righteousness..." – 2 Timothy 4:7–8 (KJV)

From the moment Elisha received Elijah's mantle on the banks of the Jordan, he made a decision that defined the rest of his life: *to live under the power and presence of God until his last breath.* He did not merely minister in the anointing—he was saturated with it, so much so that even in death, his bones still carried the residue of divine power.

His life shouts across the centuries: The grave cannot cancel the anointing. Death could stop Elisha's heartbeat, but it could not silence God's work through him. And that same truth is available for every believer who yields fully to the call of God.

Living Beyond Your Years

We often measure life by years, but God measures life by impact. The real question is not How long did you live? But what will continue to live because you lived for God?

When the dead man in **2 Kings 13:21** stood to his feet, he became living proof that Elisha's ministry did not end with his burial. The anointing God placed on him kept working, even when the vessel was no longer here.

That is the kind of life every believer should strive for—a life that will still be "speaking" when our voice is gone, still bearing fruit when our hands can no longer work, still influencing generations we will never meet.

The Secret to Being Anointed Until the End

1. **Stay Connected to the Source** – The anointing is not self-generated; it flows from God alone (**see John 15:5**).

2. **Guard What God Has Given You** – Don't allow compromise, pride, or distraction to contaminate the oil (**see 1 Timothy 6:20**).

3. **Pour It Out Freely** – Use your gifts, serve others, and leave nothing "buried" in you when your race is over (**see 2 Timothy 4:6**).

4. **Prepare the Next Generation** – Pass the mantle intentionally so the work of God continues after you (**see Psalm 145:4**).

Finishing Well

The Apostle Paul could say, **"I have fought a good fight... I have kept the faith"** because he stayed faithful to his assignment until the very end. Finishing well is not about never facing setbacks—it's about never quitting your call.

Elisha's last miracle was proof that faithfulness to God is never wasted. Even when it looks like your season is over, God can still use what you've left behind to bring life to others.

Your Legacy Is Your Real Testimony

When you are gone, your possessions will be distributed, your titles forgotten, and your name perhaps remembered by a few—but the impact of your obedience to God will ripple into eternity. That's the legacy that matters.

> **"Blessed are the dead which die in the Lord... that they may rest from their labours; and their works do follow them." – Revelation 14:13 (KJV)**

The question is not whether you will leave something behind—you will. The question is, will it bring people closer to God?

Final Charge

Live so saturated in God's presence that His anointing will outlast you.

Love so deeply that your prayers will still be answered long after you are gone.

Serve so faithfully that your life becomes a testimony others want to follow.

And when the day comes for you to step into eternity, may it be said of you: *They were anointed until the end...and beyond.*

Declaration of Legacy

I declare that my life belongs fully to the Lord Jesus Christ. I will guard the anointing, walk in obedience, and pour myself out for His glory. My race will be run with faithfulness, my calling fulfilled with courage, and my legacy will point generations to the living God. The grave will not silence my testimony, for the anointing of the Lord will outlive me. Amen.

SCRIPTURE REFERENCE INDEX

The Anointing's Source and Nature

- Exodus 29:7
- Exodus 31:3
- 1 Samuel 16:13
- Isaiah 61:1
- John 15:5
- 1 John 2:27
- 2 Corinthians 3:5

The Endurance of the Anointing

- 2 Kings 2:9–15
- 2 Kings 13:20–21
- Romans 11:29
- Revelation 14:13
- Psalm 92:10

God's Timing and Unlikely Moments

- Ecclesiastes 3:1
- Exodus 3:1–4
- Judges 6:11–12
- Luke 5:2–10
- 1 Corinthians 2:5
- Psalm 31:15

Legacy and Spiritual Inheritance

- Proverbs 10:7
- Isaiah 1:19
- Mark 10:45
- Psalm 27:4
- Proverbs 13:22
- 2 Timothy 2:2
- Judges 2:10
- Psalm 78:4

Revival and Awakening

- Ephesians 5:14
- Revelation 3:1–2
- Hosea 10:12
- Joel 2:12–13
- Acts 4:31
- Psalm 85:6
- Matthew 25:1–13

The Impossible Made Possible

- Jeremiah 32:27
- Genesis 18:10–14
- Exodus 14:21–22
- Joshua 6:20
- Matthew 14:17–21
- John 11:43–44
- Romans 4:19–21
- 1 Corinthians 15:55

Last-Day Graveyard Miracles

- Ezekiel 37:3–10
- Isaiah 60:1
- Matthew 9:37
- Habakkuk 2:14
- John 11:39–44

Finishing Well

- 2 Timothy 4:6–8
- Philippians 1:6
- Matthew 6:19–20